Investing Wisely

A Systematic Approach to Residential

Real Estate Investment

First Edition

Alan Lee

Copyright © 2017 by Venture Quarters. All rights reserved.

No part of this publication may be reproduced, distributed, or transmitted in any form or by any means, including photocopying, recording, or other electronic or mechanical methods, without the prior written permission of the publisher. For permission requests, email to the publisher at alan@venturequarters.com.

Limit of Liability/Disclaimer of Warranty: While the publisher and author have used their best efforts in preparing this book, they make no representations or warranties with respect to the accuracy or completeness of the contents of this book and specifically disclaim any implied warranties of merchantability or fitness for a particular purpose. No warranty may be created or extended by sales representatives or written sales materials. The advice and strategies contained herein may not be suitable for your situation. You should consult with a professional where appropriate. Neither the publisher nor author shall be liable for any loss of profit or any other commercial damages, including but not limited to special, incidental, consequential, or other damages.

Residential Real Estate Investment: Straight to the Point

First Edition: December 2017

Chapter 7
Building your network and scaling it out 79

Chapter 8
Check List 89

Introduction

Who am I and why did I write this book?

Hello my fellow real estate investors! My name is Alan and I began my journey into real estate investment over a year ago. Like many others, I was overwhelmed with an endless amount of information. I read books, searched online forums, and traveled across the country to research real estate. Eventually, after acquiring nearly a dozen properties across the country, my friends grew interested in my investment strategy. I began gathering material to educate my friends when I realized that most available material were either overly comprehensive or too basic. Here, I share with you a collection of my personal notes that cover the essentials of real estate investment, allowing you to acquire properties in a systematic approach.

I was born in Michigan and graduated from the University of Michigan with a degree in Computer Engineering, before moving to San Jose, California to start a career in software engineering. I have held multiple software engineering and management positions throughout Silicon Valley, including Cisco, PlaySpan (acquired by Visa), and most currently at Apple. In addition, I founded a learning management software start-up with a focus on enabling academic growth.

So why did I pick real estate investment? As many of you know, income diversity is important to a healthy financial life and protects against economic uncertainty. This typically means investing in various stocks, mutual funds, bonds, and even lower interest savings accounts. However, all of these investments have one thing in common; you have no control over the success of the company. Excluding the ultra-wealthy, you will never have enough stock ownership to make difference in these companies. If you are like me, putting all your hard earned money into the hands of a corporation and hoping it grows, is unappealing.

I found interest in real estate after seeing tremendous growth in the San Jose area. Everywhere I looked, I saw incredible potential for financial gain with the ability to control your own destiny. You determine your rent price, decide upgrades to the house to increase the rental income, and you create strategies for a small team to help you acquire more properties. You feel like a business owner and although it takes quite some initial work, the rewards are abundant.

Over the past year, I wrote software to help me locate investable properties. As of the writing of this book, I have not completed the software for public use, but if you are interested in using or testing the software, please feel free to email me at alan@venturequarters.com.

I intend for this book to be a quick read, straight to the point, with no filler to meet page requirements. I hope to share with you the necessary information and tools to purchase your investment property.

I would like to thank my friends David and Leslie for graciously providing input on my book and assisting with the editing.

Who should read this book?

If you are looking to get into residential real estate investment, focused on single family, condo, and townhouses and are looking for the tools and knowledge necessary to make an informed decision, then this is your book. I will give you the necessary background to start investing, but you may still have to do homework on certain subjects. My goal is to make this book readable in a single sitting to arm you with enough knowledge to begin your journey into real estate investment.

If you have any questions please feel free to reach me at alan@venturequarters.com or any of the below channels.

🐦 @VentureQuarters

📷 @VentureQuarters

f @VentureQuarters

Chapter 1
Why invest in real estate?

Growth

Investing in residential property is not an easy task. The stakes are high and you need to be confident with your analysis before you purchase a home. However, once you understand the core purchasing metrics, buying properties become a less daunting task.

Let's look at an example to understand investment growth. Imagine you purchased a $250,000 house in the Dallas, Texas area. Historically, homes in this neighborhood grew 8% annually and with this continued trajectory, your $250,000 asset grows to $367,000 in 5 years. Not bad, but there are plenty of investments that grow faster, including the S&P 500 index. So where is the real financial gain? Presuming the home was mortgaged at 20% down payment, your initial cash investment was only $50,000. You grew $50,000 into $117,000 over the 5 year period. Additionally, when you factor in rent and principal pay off, you net another $22,000 over 5 years to drive your investment value to $139,000. Finally, a conservative 3% annual return on top of your $50,000 investment from rental income minus total expenses earns an additional $7,500 over 5 years, bringing your final value to $146,500. Barring tax advantages and miscellaneous expenditures, you have transformed $50,000 into $146,500, a 300%

increase over 5 years, or 24% annually. Comparing the S&P 10% annualized return, your $50,000 investment only grows to $80,000 over the same 5 year period.

The reason why you accelerated your gains was because you borrowed money to purchase the house, also known as leverage. The 8% property gain applies to the entire $250,000 house value even though you only invested $50,000. The equivalent investment in the stock market is margins trading. However, margins' trading typically involves short-term holdings, due to high interest rates and inherent risk of trading stocks. When your tenants pay your mortgage, this is equivalent to dividend payments for your stock. Think of real estate investment as a dividend returning stock that you are purchasing on margins that is a lower risk and long term holding.

When you invest in properties, you can choose the rent, upgrade the property to increase home value, or lower cost by finding cost effective property managers. This leads us to the second reason for real estate investment.

Control

When you purchase stock, you place money in the hands of macroeconomic conditions and self-motivated company executives. You have little control over the company's operations, unless you own a significant portion of equity. You can only control when to buy and sell as you hope to catch the market wave at the right time.

They are key advantages when it comes to real estate investments. The rental market is much more stable. Even during the 2008 market, the DOW Jones Industrial Index fell 54% while the rental market stayed steady. Outside of macro economic conditions, you have control over your property earnings. You can choose to upgrade the property to increase the rental and sale price. You can continue to lower your cost, by purchasing additional properties, which reduces your property management fees or you can find more cost effective property managers. You can refinance your mortgage to a lower interest rate which lowers your monthly payments and increases your cash flow. You can also choose to increase your rent during strong economic conditions.

Personally, I enjoy having this investment control, which allows me to steer the financial outcome.

Cash Flow

Depending on the risk and effort applied to your portfolio, cash flow is a real possibility. On the real estate investment spectrum, you have growth on one end and cash flow on the other. Your risk tolerance will determine where you stand on this spectrum. Your stance may differ as you acquire multiple properties. Let's define each side of the spectrum.

You have growth when a property value increase quickly, but does not necessarily provide you with month-to-month cash. An example would be investment properties in San Jose, California. Here, you can receive $3,000 in rent on a $900,000 home. On a 20% mortgage, you will be spending a significant amount, since the expenses will exceed the rent. However, property values soared by 73% over the past 5 years, because of its central location in Silicon Valley, where money has poured in from technology companies. This is the growth side of the spectrum, because house prices have increased significantly, but lacked cash flow.

You have positive cash flow when rental income exceeds the expenses. An example can be found in San Antonio, Texas, where you can purchase homes for $280,000 and rent them for $2,200. Compared to San Jose, you can purchase three properties, have money to spare, and bring in nearly $6,600 in rent (the rent from 3 properties combined). However, in San Antonio, the average growth was only 47% during the same 5 year period. This is the cash flow side of the spectrum, where you receive more rental income, but less property growth.

I typically stay cash flow positive and similar to stocks, I diversify my properties across the spectrum. The advantage of positive cash flows is scaling out and acquiring more properties, without having to compound expenses. Additionally, it buffers for economic downtowns, where rental rates could drop. The advantage of growth properties is a larger return on your investment.

Drawbacks

Real estate investment has its drawbacks. Because of its high startup cost compared to stock market investments, you need significant knowledge regarding the local economy, property acquisition process, and metrics for an investable property. Similar to purchasing stocks, if you were investing $50,000 into a single stock, you would do significantly more research prior to investment. The advantage of stock market investments is the smaller financial risk and ability to sell, even in losses. With a property, when property values fall significantly, you cannot sell at losses without making up the difference in cash or taking a credit hit.

It is easier to diversify your stocks compared to real estate, especially if you are only investing in a few properties. Lastly, property investments are much less liquid, which describes the ability to turn assets into cash for immediate use. You can quickly sell shares of stocks and have access to cash within a few business days. With a property, it may take months to find a buyer before you can turn your property into cash. The other way to quickly pull cash out of a property is to open a home equity line of credit. The process can take a month, but you can request for a larger amount and only use the cash as you need it. Remember, that the cash is borrowed against your property so you will pay interest defined by the bank.

Real estate investment rewards patient investors who are willing to hold property over several years.

Summary

I encourage you to diversify your finances across stocks, bonds, real estate, and even savings accounts. You also need long term investments that grow significantly, such as real estate. Shorter term investments allow you to get cash quickly, such as stocks, bonds, and savings accounts.

Chapter 2

The two most important formulas

Cash-on-Cash and Debt-to-Income Ratio

The two most important formulas in residential real estate investment is cash-on-cash and debt-to-income ratio. Cash-on-cash allows you to visualize the return on investment from your initial cash investment. Debt-to-income ratio calculates your borrowing power from conventional lenders. Let's dig into each of these algorithms.

Cash-on-Cash

Perhaps the most important formula in residential property investment is cash-on-cash. Let's analyze the equation:

$$CashOnCash = \frac{AnnualRevenue - AnnualExpense}{InitialCost}$$

The top portion of the formula represents gross profit, while the bottom half represents the acquisition cost of the property. The top portion is commonly known as cash flow, a terminology used extensibly in this book. Think of cash flow as the amount of additional cash in your bank account at year end and cash-on-cash as the percentage growth on your initial down payment. I will discuss this topic more in this chapter.

Before discussing the formula components in depth, let's review the non-contributing factors. We do not factor in principle pay down and tax write-offs. Why? Because we are interested in the amount of liquid cash being generated by the property. If your cash-on-cash is 0%, this means you can own the property without needing additional funds after the purchase. This is increasingly important when owning many properties. A positive cash-on-cash represents the profit percentage you are generating on the initial investment. A negative cash-on-cash represents the percentage of the initial investment that you need to pay annually to own the property. Having a positive cash-on-cash provides a safety net by creating a buffer between rent prices and expenses.

Remember, just because your cash-on-cash is zero does not mean you are not making money. The principle is being paid down and the property is appreciating in value. Personally, I target as little as 2 to 3% cash-on-cash for higher end houses including property management fees. You will see an example later in the chapter where even small cash-on-cash can mean large growth.

Cash Flow

A quick note on cash-on-cash versus cash flow. You may see them used interchangeably, but they have different meanings. Cash-on-cash tells you the growth from the initial invested amount, while cash flow tells you the net change in cash over time. For example, if the cash-on-cash is 5% for a property, you can visualize the growth amount regardless of the property cost. If you invested $50,000 into a property, then a 5% cash-on-cash means that your investment is growing at $2,500 annually.

However, if the cash flow on a property was $1,000, it is not enough information to visualize growth because it does not consider the initial cost. If the initial investment was $10,000 then your growth is 10%, but if the initial investment was $100,000, then you only have 1% growth.

Positive cash flow means you will not have to put additional money towards the house, after the initial purchase. All expenses, such as mortgage payments, property tax, and property management are all offset by rental income. This is important as your portfolio grows. Having a positive cash flow provides you buffer during economic turmoil where rental rates can fall. A negative cash flow can require a lot of additional capital as your portfolio grows. A negative cash flow of $200 a month means a $2,400 a year deficit. Having ten properties with a $2,400 deficit for each property means $24,000 a year.

You should think of cash flow as a buffer and the amount is typically insignificant if you have a property manager. The gains come from principal pay off and property appreciation over time.

As you read, I will say positive cash flow, when the actual growth percentage is not important. Now let's see the variables that account for each part of the cash-on-cash formula.

Annual Revenue

This is the easy one. You typically have a single source of revenue for your rental property which is rental income. Simply take the monthly rent and multiply by 12 to get the annual revenue. Do not subtract any expenses.

Annual Expense

Annual expense is more complicated. This accounts for any costs incurred towards your house. Taking the revenue generated and subtracting out the annual expenses results in the cash in your account, also known as cash flow. Always aim for a positive cash flow.

So what counts towards Annual Expenses?

Mortgage

One of the biggest expenses is the mortgage. If you mortgaged the property and paid 20% down on a 30 year fixed interest rate, half of your rental income goes towards paying the mortgage. Do not subtract out principle payments; the entire mortgage amount is the expense you should consider. Because principle pay down is not a realizable gain until you either sell the home or take out a home equity loan, we must use the entire mortgage amount to figure out the immediate cash flow.

Take the monthly mortgage payment and multiply by 12 to get the annual mortgage expense.

Property Tax

Property tax is often an overlooked expense and can make or break your investment. You must check property tax rates for each property. In Northern California, there are entire counties that have flat tax rates. However, in Texas, rates can vary in neighboring areas. Never make assumptions about tax rates and use previous years property taxes to calculate expenses. I have made mistakes where I made assumptions that an entire city had the same tax rate and I discounted many investible properties. Always work with your buyer agent to get exact tax rates for a property.

In states where housing prices are high, such as Northern California, property tax rates tend to be lower. Santa Clara county which govern several cities in North California, average house prices are over $1 Million and the property tax rate is only 1.24%. However in Dallas, Houston, Austin and other areas in Texas, houses can be acquired for less than $200,000, but property tax rates range from 2% to 4%.

Property tax is normally quoted annually and is the amount you will consider for the annual expense.

Property Management

Property managers are crucial when investing in areas that are far from home. The property management cost is a significant expense in the cash-on-cash calculation. However, as you acquire more properties, managing properties become challenging especially if you are looking for passive income.

Property managers are responsible for many aspects of your investment, including tenant searches, performing background checks, coordinating with maintenance companies, collecting rent and direct deposits, and even helping to evict troublesome tenants.

You should find the property management cost for each major city, since they vary drastically. For example in San Antonio, it is common to see a 10% monthly fee ($200 monthly fee for a $2000 monthly rent) and a half-month rent for the leasing fee. However in Dallas, it is common to see a $95 flat monthly fee and one-month rent for the leasing fee. These rates vary amongst companies, so compare several companies in each area. You can find reliable property managers through Yelp, Google, or your agent.

The most important property management costs are the management fee, leasing fee and renewal fee. Management fees are paid monthly and are used to cover tenant direct deposits and maintenance calls. Leasing fee is charged each time a property manager needs to find and place a tenant. Lastly, the renewal fee is charged when the lease expires and the tenant renews. Some property managers do not charge renewal fees.

You can estimate the annual expense by taking the monthly management fee and multiplying by 12. The leasing and renewal fee expense is more difficult to account since it spans multiple years. For the investment area, check the average renter's duration. On average, renters typically stay for three years so you can expect to pay the leasing fee every three years. For calculating the annual leasing expense divide the leasing expense by 3. Lease durations are normally 12 or 24 months depending on your contract, so you can expect to pay the renewal fee every 1 or 2 years. For calculating the annual renewal expense, divide the renewal fee by 1 or 2, depending the lease terms.

The management, leasing, and renewal fees calculated above, is your annual property management expense.

Insurance

Insurance costs can make certain areas a difficult investment. This is especially true for areas that anticipate major disasters, such as hurricane prone areas. When searching for investment properties, attempting to get insurance quotes for each property is time consuming. To ensure you cash flow estimates are accurate, look for a property that is within your price range and share similar characteristics to your investment criteria. Search for several insurance companies to get competitive quotes. Normally, the quotes should be accurate for properties in similar areas and conditions. Consider using an insurance broker who is local to the investment area and can compare quotes against multiple companies to find the best rate.

Insurance rates drastically fluctuate based on climate and safety factors. For example, insurance on a $250,000 house in Houston can cost over $2500 because of hurricanes, where a similar home in Austin can cost less than $1000. In California, the only significant natural disasters is fire and earthquakes and insurance prices can be less than $1,000 to insure a $1 million dollar home.

In addition to quoting larger insurance companies like Travelers, Liberty Mutual, or Geico, try using local mortgage brokers in the investment area. In Dallas Texas, I received quotes for over $2,000 with big name insurance companies, where local mortgage brokers was able to find A+ insurance companies for only $1000. Remember to research the insurance companies online and ensure they are reputable and payout claims.

Insurance is normally quoted with an annual price which can be used for calculating the annual expense.

Homeowners Association Fees (HOA)

HOA is a small governing body run by members who live in the community in addition to a third party company, who help with funds and management of any shared public spaces. Shared public spaces include community pools, playgrounds, security, and parks. Even front lawns can be managed by HOA. HOA fees are typically several hundred dollars a year for single family property, but can be in the thousands for newer properties with a myriad of amenities. These fees can reduce several percentage points off your cash-on-cash.

HOA fees are typically paid monthly, quarterly, bi-annually, or annually so remember to extrapolate the cost into your annual expense.

Miscellaneous Expenses

All houses will run into issues that you will be responsible for fixing as a landlord. This can include plumbing, electrical, broken appliance, or any physical issue with the property. Estimating the cost can be difficult since it depends on the home conditions and a tenants ability to fix minor issues.

If your house is in a new condition, you can estimate 2% to 5% of your rental income towards maintenance. Older homes maintenance cost can easily range between 5% to 10%. When you own multiple properties, some will go years without problems and others will have issues monthly, making estimates difficult.

I tend to invest in newer homes that are renovated and do not require additional work, so I reserve 2% to 5% of my rental income for maintenance. Remember to amortize the expense annually.

Initial Cost

Now to the 3rd and final piece of the equation. Initial cost is the initial cash investment into the property. Let's see which items are considered initial cost.

Down payment

The down payment is the largest portion of the initial cost. I prefer 20% down so I can use my assets towards acquiring more properties. For a $300,000 property, the down payment would be $60,000 at 20%.

There are a few other items that account for the initial cost. Recall that initial costs are one-time payments and are not expected to repeat.

Closing Cost

These are costs incurred by the lender to process your loan. This includes points to buy down your rate (I will tell you about this more later) and fees for processing the loan. These costs can typically be negotiated with lenders and closing costs can vary amongst lenders.

You can expect closing cost to be around $3000 to $4000 when borrowing $200,000. Most costs associated to closing cost is static and does not increase as you borrow more money. If you borrowed $400,000, the closing cost is not necessarily $6000 to $8000. Your lender can provide you with an estimated closing cost during the initial loan process. When reading the final closing documents, which I will discuss further in the book, many values should not be counted towards closing costs, such as prepaid for insurance, HOA, or property tax since they are accounted for in the annual expenses. These expenses are included in the final closing cost, but you should remove them as part of the cash flow calculation.

When shopping around for lenders, ask them for the estimated closing cost and only factor in the origination cost, appraisal fees, and title fees. These should be the administrative cost to process the loan.

The closing cost is added to the down payment for calculating the initial cost.

Property Enhancement Cost

If you are buying a property that requires major enhancements, you should count them towards the initial cost. These may include carpet replacement, kitchen renovations, paint jobs and appliance servicing. This cost can be difficult to estimate without a home inspection. The seller disclosure that the agent provides should always be reviewed since it should contain known major issues. Also, after your offer is accepted and a professional has inspected the home, you can work with contractors to get an accurate cost. An approximate estimate after reviewing the seller disclosure and visual inspection by your agent should be sufficient. Unlike the annual expenses, estimating a higher initial cost will insignificantly impact the cash-on-cash calculation.

Now you might ask, how do you factor in major renovations in 15 to 20 years, as part of the cash flow calculation now? Hopefully, the 2% to 5% that was set aside for maintenance is not entirely consumed and some of it can be used for these enhancements. Estimating costs 15 to 20 years in the future can be challenging. You may completely renovate a kitchen costing $20,000 to $30,000 in twenty years. However, your goal is to calculate a cash-on-cash return to ensure that you have buffer money for the near-term, where the risk is at it's highest. Twenty years from now, you should have significant equity in the home and major investments to fix the property, will only increase the home value when sold. You may chose to sell the house as-is and realize the gains immediately without fixes. Although, you should always purchase homes in faster growing areas when possible, the cash-on-cash calculation does not estimate future growth and expenses.

Example

Now that we have established the equation parameters, let's take a look at an example calculation from my first property. It will showcase the desire for positive cash flow, even if the annual amount is insignificant.

$$CashOnCash = \frac{AnnualRevenue - AnnualExpense}{InitialCost}$$

Equation Variable	Event	Amount	Annual Amount
AnnualRevenue	Rent	2195 / month	26,340
Total Annual Revenue			26,340
AnnualExpense	Mortgage	1202.36 / month	14,428.32
AnnualExpense	Property Tax	6466.21 / year	6466.21
AnnualExpense	Property Management	195 / month	2,340
AnnualExpense	Insurance	913 / year	913

Equation Variable	Event	Amount	Annual Amount
AnnualExpense	HOA	466 / year	466
AnnualExpense	Misc	500 / year	500
Total Annual Expense			25,113.53
InitialCost	Down Payment (20%)	56,800	
InitialCost	Closing Cost	5218.56	
Total Initial Cost			62,018.56
Cash on Cash			1.98%

$$1.98\% = \frac{26{,}340 - 25{,}113.53}{62{,}018.56} \cdot 100$$

Looking at these number, there's nothing to brag about pocketing $1226.47 a year with a cash-on-cash of 1.98%. I treat the $1226.47 cash flow as a buffer for unexpected expenses or poor economic conditions. I can lower the rent by $100 a month, before I break even. Once your portfolio grows large, having many negative cash flow properties, will require you to pay large sums of money to own the properties. So what are the upsides of owning the property after only making $1226.47 in cash the first year? After a year with this property, the value went up by $20,000 and $3425 of the principal has been paid off. That is approximately $24,651 gain on the initial

$62,018.56 investment, which is nearly a 40% return on my initial investment!

Now let's talk about one last equation that you need in your back pocket.

Debt-to-Income Ratio

The second equation that you must remember is the debt-to-income ratio (DTI). This ratio dictates the maximum loan amount for purchasing homes under common loan conditions. This ratio is commonly referred to as DTI.

$$DTI = \frac{Sum\,of\,all\,Debt}{Sum\,of\,All\,Income}$$

DTI is a simple fraction. The numerator is the sum of all debt and the denominator is the sum of all income. When borrowing money through most banks and lenders, the loans are typically resold to Fannie Mae, Freddie Mac, or guaranteed by the FHA. This requires the lender to follow strict guidelines, including the borrower having a specific DTI, so they can easily resell the loan.

Having a low DTI means you have low debt compared to your income, and having lower debt means you are more likely to pay your loans. A person, who has high debt relative to their income, has a higher risk of missing loan payments, especially if their debt increases or their income falls.

So why is DTI important? When borrowing money to buy homes, the guidelines stipulate that you can borrow up to 45% of your income. So if you earn $120,000 annually, your income is $10,000 a month, which allows you $4,500 worth of monthly debt. This debt includes mortgages, car payments, alimony, credit cards, property tax, and most significant bills. The mortgage company is ensuring that you are not spending beyond your means. Some lenders, such as portfolio lenders, will lend to individuals even when their DTI exceeds 45%. This translates to higher interest rates, since the loan cannot be sold to Fannie Mae, and must be held by the lender or sold to high risk mortgage companies.

What is considered debt and income?

Debt

Debt include all significant expenditures. This includes existing mortgages, loans, credit card bills, insurance bills, child support, property tax, etc. The loan officer will run credit checks and request for all bills and statements for the previous months to verify expenses. If you apply for loans or credit cards, the lender will request for an explanation of the credit request. You will not be penalized as long as additional debt is not incurred. During the loan process, the future home loan is factored into the debt calculations. In the above example where you earn $120,000 annually, if you have $4,500 worth of monthly debt and you are applying for a loan that results in $2,000 payments, your DTI becomes 65%. You must lower your debt to qualify for a loan.

Income

What counts as income can be tricky. A salary job is an easy income calculation. Your income comprises of a salary plus any bonuses and tips. Rental income, stock dividends, and social security are also considered. You can approximate your debt and income, but exact values will require a lenders calculation. Some forms of income, like stock dividends and tips, can vary year over year and the lender will decide the income calculations. Note, any income fluctuations over two years, especially if it drops, will likely require an explanation.

Some companies provide employee retention payments in the form of stock units and these are tricky to calculate. Since, stock value can fluctuate quickly, different lenders will calculate stock as income differently. In fact, some lenders do not treat stock grants as income. Verify with lender during the pre-qualification phase, on whether stock grants can be counted as income. Otherwise, you may need to look for another lender, especially if your DTI is reaching 45%. Lenders will only consider a percentage of the stock vested in a calendar year as income and they prefer to see the grants continuously replenished by your company. Each lender considers stock income differently. Some will use the average vested value, whereas others will use the lowest stock price for the year. You want a lender who can maximize your income, especially if you plan to acquire multiple properties.

Debt-to-Income

Now that you understand debt and income, divide your total monthly debt and your total monthly income to estimate your DTI. If you are close to 45%, you may have problems securing your next loan, but work with your lender and see how you might qualify, by paying off some debt. Lenders can take future rental income to lower your DTI. Otherwise, you will need to explore investment property lenders. If your DTI is low, work with a lender to pre-qualify for a loan. Based on a few debt and income estimates, they will be able to provide you the maximum loan amount.

Understanding DTI is important, but I do not recommend calculating it on your own. Lenders consider many other factors and your estimates can be off. Always consult your lender who can provide you with a more accurate estimate.

Cash-on-Cash and Debt-to-Income ratio are the two most critical formulas in this book. Now, lets try to find a home!

Chapter 3
How to find a property?

Preparation

Understanding the criteria of a good investment is critical when you need to make a fast decision. Cash-on-cash ensures you have a solid financial return and we must use those fundamentals to find strong properties.

Good properties will sell quickly by investors and non-investors. When I started residential property investment, I looked at over fifty properties before putting in an offer. Sometimes, you run into counter offer situations and knowing the numbers will allow you to make quick decisions to either counter or move on. In hot markets, making quick decisions is a key to success.

This chapter will focus on finding the right property and setting up relationships with agents, property managers, and lenders so you can find properties remotely.

Finding the area

Armed with the math behind property investments, it is time to start researching. Narrowing down a few investable cities or area is the first task at hand. The reason I mentioned area in addition to a city, is because many larger cities are surrounded by smaller cities, that are more affordable and have similar growth patterns. Searching for an investable area will require a lot of research.

There is no perfect area and your risk tolerance can favor certain areas over others. You may prefer San Jose because of the booming tech economy. You may prefer Austin or Boston, because it has a tech economy, but less established than San Jose, making it more affordable but still in a high growth area. You might avoid New York because of the frigid weather and afraid of the wear and tear that it brings. This book cannot advise you on investable areas simply because there is no correct answer. As booming as San Jose or Silicon Valley might be, a small single family house averages for over $1 million and the cash flow is negative at 20% down payment. Unless you have significant capital, San Jose will not be an investable city for most.

There are a few key things when searching for investable areas. Start by researching major cities in each state and read Wikipedia articles on economic conditions. Personally, I was looking for areas with that had a diversified economy. Because I am familiar with the technology industry, I searched for areas with a tech economy. If you are familiar with the oil or finance sector other cities with those economies maybe preferable. You should search for cities or areas within economic sectors that you are familiar with to help gauge the potential city growth.

Population growth is an important factor. Wikipedia Demographics section provides census and historical population growth. Cities that attract people typically means strong economic conditions and favorable living conditions. The demographic section also provides median household incomes that can help gauge the populations buying power.

Climate conditions was a major factor in my decisions since I preferred to avoid areas with frequent natural disasters. Natural disasters increase the insurance cost, maintenance cost and can result in a higher risk portfolio. Some of these areas can have significant cash flow, but I was not willing to risk a major disaster. Others who are less risk aversive could find potential gains in these areas.

I did the typical Google searches for "Top Cities to Own Investment Properties" and only used those as a starting point. The results are typically too broad and used high level revenue and expense estimates that do not guarantee cash flow. I utilized real estate applications such as Zillow and Redfin to estimate home affordability and rental estimates. Both Zillow and Redfin provides purchase price estimates and Zillow provides rental estimates. After a bit of searching, my research favored areas with high population, economies driven by high technology, good school districts, and sunny areas with minimum natural disasters. Again, there are many investable areas outside of these criteria. Similar to stock investment, people tend to invest in the sector where they are employed, since they are familiar with the domain and economic conditions.

Other criteria to consider include crime rates, quality of schools, and housing conditions. Google street view can even give you a virtual tour of neighborhoods. Remember that your goal is to find investable areas where the houses align with your budget and match your investment criteria. Do not worry about calculating exact cash flows yet since that requires a deeper dive.

Come up with a list of Top 3 area before performing deep dives in them. Deep dives are time consuming since you will need to research property management, insurance companies, and real estate agents. These deep dives help with accurate cost estimation. Let's see how we can perform deep dives.

House Criteria

Housing prices fluctuate based on many factors. You may prioritize different factors based on personal taste and investment strategy. For example, being in top rated school district will raise home prices. Many other factors raise home prices including shorter commutes to work, low crime rates, walking distance to shopping areas, amongst many others. Let's review some of the common investment criteria.

Houses close to city downtowns are typically more costly. Because of closer commutes to work or night life, property value are typically higher and increase faster. There is typically high demand for these properties so finding renters will be very easy. There are drawbacks for being closer to downtown areas. Since downtown areas are normally highly developed, single family homes can be difficult to find and you may have to settle for smaller condominiums. Condos have shared land amongst all property owners, which translates to limited land value. A single family home on a plot of land and can be expanded and modernized, whereas condos are part of a larger structure and only the internals can be updated. Downtown areas attract younger renters where as the suburbs attract families with kids. If you are looking in a downtown area and the homes are too costly for the size, you may need to explore the suburbs to find newer, larger, and cheaper properties.

School districts is a very important consideration for renters with families, which should be part of your investment strategy. Homes in good school districts are highly sought out by families and increase their value quicker. Location versus school district are examples of why there is never a "best area" for investment. If you prefer higher growth and demand, then you may prefer downtowns. If you prefer homes with more land, good school districts, and family renters, then you may prefer suburbs.

The age of a home is another important consideration. Insurance rates tend to increase with older homes. Older homes that need work, will increase the initial property cost and decrease the cash-on-cash calculations. Older properties is typically cheaper than a comparable newer property, which can help if you are looking to stay in a budget. Installing new carpet, painting, and modernizing a home is expensive so consult a handy man to estimate these costs to calculate your cash flow. Often times, you can get great deals on older properties that need minimal work. Investing a few thousand dollars into a home can be worth the time and effort, if the property is in a good area with rising property values and rent.

With older homes, watch out for foundation and structural problems which are very expensive to fix. During the agent walk-through have them look for cracks and foundation separation. They can easily spot major structural deficiencies and home conditions, which do not show up in real estate pictures.

There are many other criteria that can impact home values. Some include vicinity to busy roads, power lines, open concept lay out, granite countertops, and lot size. No house is perfect and few will match all of your desires so determine which criteria are the most important. Personally, having good schools, an open concept living room, and natural lighting are must haves for my properties.

Find an agent

Having a trustworthy agent will make your buying experience much easier. As you filter through properties, a good agent will start recommending properties that fit your taste. Your agent will search for properties while you are busy, so make sure they understand your search criteria. I always have my agents call me, if they find a great deal on a property that meet most of my criteria, so I can write same day offers.

A word of warning. Do not let agents coerce you into purchasing properties that do not cash flow. Often times, agents calculate cash flow without having correct estimates for property management, insurance, and other expenses. You get presented with cash-on-cash percentages that are much higher than in reality. I have my agents provide cash-on-cash calculations based on my cost estimates. Always do your own homework!

You can try sites like Zillow, Realtor, or Redfin for finding an agent, which also includes agent reviews. Zillow has an agent finder that filter based on languages, home types, and specific areas. I have found several of my agents through Zillow. Google your agents name and see if you can find reviews on the internet.

Two very important characteristic of an agent is patience and having a sense of urgency. They need to be willing to visit properties, send video recordings, and provide you data points on a property to enable quick decision making. Your agent should be patient and not force you into buying a home quickly to get their commission. Your agent should also have a sense of urgency. I have seen good deals fall through because agents were slow to react. Do not be afraid to switch agents if you sense that they are impatient, want to make a quick sale, or do not respond quickly to your communication.

Always provide your agent with direct and honest feedback. If you do not like a home, tell them the reasons so they can improve their listings. This feedback will enable a more efficient property search. Also, ensure that your agent is providing you positive and negative feedback on all properties. Remember, you are not there to smell the house, see cracks on the walls, and hear the outside road noises. If your agent is constantly pressuring you into deals or hiding property issues from you, it is time for a new agent.

A question that I am asked often is whether they should partner with a junior or senior real estate agent. A seasoned agent can be helpful if you are new to investing and require a lot of input. They can provide input in investable areas, school district boundaries, and can spot good deals quickly. Junior agents can be more energetic and patient and can provide you with more attention. Personally, I have a mix of junior and senior real estate agents. My junior agents are very responsive at all hours of the day, which help a lot since I am investing across timezones. I also have senior agents in areas where I am less knowledgeable. Personally, regardless of an agents seniority they must be flexible with their hours and have a sense of urgency.

Once you discover an investable property, request your agent for a video walk through immediately. They should record every room, the back yard, and the front view.

Properties sell quick in strong markets so your agent should react quickly. Have them note down any smells in the house, the general condition of every room, traffic noise, power lines, natural lighting, etc.

If you plan to purchase multiple properties, you must have a trustworthy agent to find and secure quick deals.

Mortgage Loan Officer and a Pre-qualification

A mortgage loan officer is responsible for securing your loan and coordinates the sale with your agent and title company. Having a strong loan officer enables you to purchase multiple homes quickly since they will already have your financial documents. Unlike a real estate agent, where you need one per area, loan officers can be licensed in multiple states and can service you across state boundaries. Let's see what makes a good mortgage loan officer.

Rates! Mortgage rates vary per lender. Check with large lenders like Wells Fargo, Chase, Bank of America, and also small lenders local to your investing area. I found my lenders through Yelp and Google searches and I currently use a single lender for all properties. When requesting rates from various lenders, ensure that the quote is with 0 discount points. Lenders will often quote lower rates, but include discount points to make their offer appear competitive. Discount points are fees paid to buy a lower mortgage rate. If a lender provides a rate that will cost 1 point, it means that you need to pay 1% of the mortgage amount to get that rate. For example, if you are borrowing $200,000 and the lender states that the rate is 4.75% with 1 discount point, you must pay $2,000 to borrow the $200,000 at 4.75%. To compare rates between lenders, ensure that all the quotes have the same terms. Normally, I compare lenders against 30 year fixed with 0 discount points on 20% down.

Another loan program that only some lenders offer for investment is adjustable rate mortgage, commonly known as ARM. ARM rates have a 5,7 or 10 year rate that is lower than 30 year fixed rates, but adjusts to market rate after the specified term. A 5-1 ARM means that the rate is locked for 5 years and then adjusts to the market rate every 1 year after. Because of the higher risk associated with ARM rates, banks offer an introductory rate that is lower than a 30 year fixed. ARM programs can be beneficial if rates do not fluctuate or you plan to sell your property before the introductory rate expires.

Rates are not the only criteria when picking a lender. Lenders could provide special loan programs. ARM programs are only available to some lenders and many lenders require 25% down for investment mortgages. Most lenders do not include vested company stocks, commonly known as RSU, as income. If your company provides RSU grants and you need it to count towards income to lower your DTI, make sure to search for lenders who understand these special income types.

Should you borrow from larger banks or smaller lenders? Larger banks have the advantage when it comes to convenient payment portals, rate matching against competitors, and reliability. However, their closing times can be longer because of their large loan volumes.

Smaller credit unions and mortgage loan officers can be more attentive to your needs and close quicker due to lower mortgage volumes. Smaller lenders that I work with will take my calls early in the morning or late at night and even on the weekends, to adjust for my schedule. I have successfully rushed several closings because I needed to leave for vacation. Most smaller lenders will provide competitive rates, if you have an offer letter from another bank.

Investment loan rates are typically higher by half a percentage due to the inherent risk of investments. Even though the rates are higher, investment loans allow you to count the future rental income to offset the debt, causing a smaller rise in your DTI. Recall that your DTI cannot exceed 45% when borrowing from conventional lenders.

After you find your lender, get a pre-qualification letter. A pre-qualification is a quick calculations of your income and expenses to estimate your maximum loan amount while staying under the DTI guidelines. A pre-qualification is not a loan guarantee. You can only guarantee a loan after you have placed an offer on a house and are in the loan process. Verifying your assets and income is a costly and time consuming process and this cannot be done as part of the pre-qualification. The more information you disclose about your income and assets during the pre-qual process, the more likely your loan will be approved.

I typically print a new pre-qual letter for each home offer to match the offer amount so that seller is not aware of my maximum loan amount. Knowing the maximum loan amount may encourage a higher counter offer. You can request for a self-modifiable document so you can change the offer amount yourself.

Property Manager

A good property manager enables passive rental income. Start searching for a property manager during your property search, so you can accurately estimate your cash flow. Property managers in different cities can have varying cost. Because property management cost is one of the highest fees that you will pay, cities with lower fees can be more investable. I have mistakenly excluded cities for investment after seeing lower rental rates, until I researched and discovered that the lower property management rates balanced out the lower rent.

For example, rental rates in San Antonio are typically higher than Dallas. In San Antonio, property managers commonly charge a 50% leasing fee and 10% monthly fee. A rental for $2000 a month will have $200 monthly fee. However in Dallas, property managers commonly charge a 50% leasing and a $95 flat monthly fee. After accounting for the cheaper property managements in Dallas, the cash flow is only marginally lower, which makes the city a great investment even with lower rent.

Property managers within a city or metropolitan typically have similar cost structures. You do not need to search for a property manager in every nearby city. Most property managers will service nearby cities and also provide discounts for multiple properties.

Google and Yelp are great resources for discovering highly rated property managers. Your real estate agent can provide property managers referrals as well. Often times, you may get better property management rates through a referral. I have found several of my property managers through Google, Yelp, and referrals, which have all turned out great.

Property managers have many costs. Here are the typical costs to inquire about:

1. Leasing Fee - This is the cost for tenant searches, open houses, background checks, and listing your properties across web portals. This normally ranges from 50% to 100% of 1 month rent. Rarely you will find management companies that have no leasing fee and those who do earn their revenue from other fees such as technology or per trip fees. Newer homes that do not require much attention can benefit from zero leasing fee, even if the per trip fee is high.

2. Management fee - This is the fee for managing your property on a monthly basis. This includes

managing maintenance calls, payment management, direct deposits, monthly statements, and evictions. Management fees are normally a percentage of the monthly rent or a flat monthly fee.

3. Renewal Fee - This is a fee for lease renewal. This is normally a flat fee and some property managers perform renewals for free.

4. Repair Markup Fee - Some property managers add an additional markup charged by a maintenance person. The fee is normally 10% of the maintenance cost. My experience is that most places do not charge this fee unless the leasing and management fees are low.

5. Property Visit Fee - This is a fee paid when you request for a property manager to visit your property. You may need them to open doors for delivery or property checkups. This is an uncommon fee, but some places use it if their leasing and management fees are low.

Based on the age and the type of renters in your property, some fee types maybe more beneficial than others. Property managers who have lower leasing fees, but have higher repair markup and property visit fee would be beneficial for newer properties, where the frequency of property visits are low. Older properties with constant maintenance will benefit with higher leasing fees and lower repair markup and property visit fees. I normally purchase newer rental homes, so property managers with a cheaper leasing and management fee, even if their repair and property visit fees are much higher, are financially beneficial.

Check the property managers reviews on Google or Yelp. Irresponsible and unresponsive property managers can drive away tenants. Property managers should answer their phones and emails promptly at all times. I have switched property managers due to unresponsiveness.

Experienced property managers will put your life at ease, especially when your portfolio grows. Experienced property management companies manage several hundred properties, while maintaining excellent customer service. Less experienced property management companies are run by small teams, who are responsible for only several properties. I would not suggest these smaller management companies unless a trusted individual provides a high recommendation. Remember, your goal is to earn passive income and the tenants happiness are dependent on the reliability of your property manager.

After finding several property managers and you are comfortable with their fee structure, always negotiate the rates. Often times, the preferred property management company charges higher fees, but making them aware of competitor rates and negotiating can lower the cost. When negotiating, remember to mention that you are a property investor and that you plan to purchase several properties.

The better the property manager, the more passive the income.

Insurance

Insurance cost vary drastically between companies, so getting several quotes is advisable. Insurance cost is significant and must be taken into account when calculating cash flow. You should get accurate insurance cost estimates in your investment area. Different areas within the same city can have varying insurance rates due to crime, flood zones, and property value.

Finding an insurance company with competitive rates is time consuming and working with an insurance broker local to the investing area can simplify the search. I prefer insurance brokers, since I simply send an email with several property addresses and they respond with quotes in a few hours. Ensure that the quoted companies have A+ ratings, which is a measure of the companies financial strength. Mortgage brokers make their money directly from the insurance companies so their service is free for you. Larger insurance companies, like Geico or Travelers, require you to input information online or over the phone, which is time consuming. Yelp and Google are useful tools for locating highly rated insurance brokers.

It is time consuming to get insurance quotes for each potential properties. Similar properties in an area should have the same insurance rates, so a single quote should be sufficient. Get an exact insurance quote prior to making an offer.

Here is another reason to get insurance quotes early in your research. When I first began my real estate endeavors, I saw great returns in Houston, especially in the Lake Houston area. Immediately before I started writing offers, I called several insurance companies to inquire about rates. After contacting several insurance companies, many of them did not insure the area, because of hurricane and flooding concerns. I dropped that area from my investment list after failing to secure a reputable insurance company.

Talking with insurance companies informs you a lot about a city. Areas with cheap rates tend to have fewer natural disasters. Houston has higher rates in certain areas due to hurricanes and flooding. Comparatively, Austin has lower rates because it is farther inland and rarely gets impacted by severe weather. Always research abnormally high insurance rates and check if they are weather related. Real estate is a long term investment that needs to sustain for many years.

Property Tax

Property tax is the most significant cost next to the mortgage. Property tax can vary within neighboring areas and having the exact amount is necessary for cash flow estimates. This information is easy to retrieve and your agent should provide it with every listing. And because property tax is one of the most significant cost, having inaccurate estimates is the difference between negative and positive cash flow.

Comparative Market Analysis (CMA)

Zillow or Redfin are great tools to get estimates on sale and rental prices. To get an accurate estimate you must request for a Comparative Market Analysis (CMA) from your agent. CMAs are sale and rental figures for a given area. Sale and rental prices can vary heavily between areas because of school zones, amenities, work commutes, etc. Your agent has access to this data through the Multiple Listings Service (MLS), and can provide the past and present sales and rental figures.

How does your agent filter out homes to provide the most accurate CMAs? They will provide you with property sales in your investment neighborhood for houses with similar square footage, property age, and in the same school district. Since timing impacts the supply and demand of properties your agent will likely only provide CMAs for the past 6 to 12 months.

Many factors drive home pricing even if they are in the same area, so treat the CMAs as an estimate. Some factors influencing the price include home conditions, home layout, lot size, amenities, supply of homes, and even natural lighting. Once you have found similar houses compared to your target property in the CMAs, the average dollar per square foot is needed to estimate your property cost. You can estimate the expected sale price of your target property by taking the dollar per square foot and multiplying it against your properties square footage. Every home is unique and market conditions can change in an instant, so treat these numbers as an estimate when calculating your offer price.

You should gather rental CMAs, so you can accurately estimate the potential rental revenue. Rental CMAs function exactly the same as sale CMAs. People rent homes and will pay differing rent based on the same criteria as the purchase of a home. One of the most important figures to inspect is the days on market. When determining your future rental price, the higher you set the rental price, the longer the property stays on the market. You should aim to have your rental on the market for at most 30 days. When looking at the CMAs, look at the rental prices in the 20 to 30 day range to figure out your target price.

Never let a property sit unrented. If you could rent out a property for $2000 immediately versus $2100 a month later, you should always choose the $2000 amount. It will take almost two years to earn back the lost wages for the month. Most lease agreements are one to two years in duration where rental rates will readjust anyways. Your property manager will also provide advice given their familiarity with the market and areas. They will gladly run a CMA for you even before you place an offer.

Putting in an Offer

Now that you are armed with an agent, the cash-on-cash algorithm, a pre-qualification letter with a mortgage loan officer, home criteria, and costs involved in a rental, you should be able to quickly calculate cash flow and make quick purchase decisions.

I plan to create a website which will include quick cash-on-cash calculations and other useful investment material. Please email me at alan@venturequarters.com for more information.

There is nothing better than a well informed decision when buying an investment property. Now let's work on putting in the offer next chapter.

Chapter 4
Putting in an offer

Finalize the numbers

You should feel confident with your cash-on-cash estimates. Gather the comparative market analysis (CMA) for both sales and rentals of the property and have all the expense estimates ready. I suggest that you calculate the cash-on-cash based on various price points so you can make quick offer adjustments. With your pre-qualification in hand, you are ready to sign offers.

Signing the Offer

Let's send out an offer. The offer signing process is very simple and they are executed electronically through a process called e-signing. You can sign an offer on your smartphone and you only need an internet connection and a copy of the pre-qualification letter. Here are some important items to observe in your offer contract.

Offer Price

The main component on the contract is the offer price. Perform a final cash flow calculation and expense validation against the offer price. When there are multiple offers and the house meets many of your criteria, you should consider a higher offer price even if it means a lower cash flow. The additional amount added into an offer is divided over a 30 year mortgage, so the monthly payments will not increase by much. Do not let a few thousand dollars stop you from investing, especially if the cash flow numbers are still favorable.

Option Fee

Options fee is a small deposit, typically $100, that removes the house from the market and allows you to hire a professional to inspect the property. During the options period, you can decline the purchase of a home and only forfeit the option fee. An options period is typically 5 to 10 days, which can be specified in the contract. The shorter the options period, the more competitive your offer will appear.

The options period is where you should setup a professional home inspection and determine the maintenance cost before proceeding with the property. I have declined to purchase homes because of structural and foundation issues uncovered during the inspection. I would rather lose the inspection and option fee, which totaled to $500 in my situation, than potentially spend thousands of dollars fixing structural issues.

Earnest Money

The earnest money is the deposit to purchase the property. You typically need to put a 1% deposit for a house. The earnest money is immediately deposited into escrow after the offer is accepted and is either applied as a credit towards the final purchase price or refunded if you revoke the offer during the option period. There is an "Approval of Financing" clause in the contract that specifies the refund of the earnest money, if your financing is not approved as well. In your contract you should specify enough time for finance approval. I normally specify 21 days for my lender, but you will need to work with your loan officer on an appropriate closing time frame.

If your loan is delayed because of your lender or you were slow to provide documentation, the seller has the right to nullify the contract and keep the earnest money. Always send your documents to the loan officer immediately to prevent delays and check on your lender progress constantly.

Title Policy

The title policy must be purchased and protects the buyer against liens discovered on the property at any time. This means at any time in the future, if someone proves to have an ownership in the property because of a mistake, the policy will protect both the buyer and the lender.

The policy amount can be negotiated so it is paid by the seller, but you can choose to pay yourself to present a stronger offer.

Survey

A home survey describes the exact property boundaries being purchased and is done by a licensed surveyor. For example, if your neighbor builds a fence onto your property line, it will be revealed in the survey. A survey must be purchased and completed.

The survey cost can be negotiated in the offer to be seller paid. You can chose to pay it, to present a stronger offer.

Home Warranty

Home warranty is an optional service and often times can be negotiated and paid by the seller. Home warranty protects your appliances, air conditioning, plumbing, washers, dryers, and other major home systems from issues for the policy duration. You can find your own home warranty company and compare their coverages online. Home warranty is normally around $500 for a year of coverage. Home warranty coverage is optional.

Closing Date

The closing date is when you and the lender transfers money to an escrow account in exchange for the house. The seller always wants to close quickly because they continue to pay the mortgage and all expenses until the property is sold. Often times, a seller will prefer a lower cash offer over a mortgaged offer because financing takes time and has a risk of getting declined.

Since most buyers will need financing, having a shorter closing time helps you strengthen the offer, but your lender must provide a feasible date. During busy times of the year, especially in the Spring and Summer, closing times will be longer. You do not want to be late with closing, since the seller has the right to deny an extension and can keep your earnest money.

Closing typically takes 30 days, but check with the lender on a realistic closing date before signing the contract.

Optional Items

Permanent items attached to the house such as dishwashers, sinks, blinds, and light fixtures are sold with the home. Some appliances such as washers, dryers, and refrigerators are not considered to be attached to the house and is not sold with the home. These items can be negotiated into the sale price if the seller does not plan to keep them. Sometimes, the owner's do not want to move large appliances and are willing to sell them for cheap or even for free.

Almost there

Now that you have submitted your offer, you will have to wait for an acceptance, counter, or rejection. You can put pressure on the seller to make a quick decision by putting a 1 or 2 day deadline on an offer. This gives the seller less time to gather other offers and increases your chances of securing the home.

If your offer is countered or rejected, work with your agent on a new offer. Remember to run your cash flow calculations against the new offer.

Once your offer is accepted, it is time for the closing process. The next chapter will dive into the various parts of the closing process.

Chapter 5
Closing the property

The Final Stretch

There is still a lot of work to do once the offer is accepted. Several fees including the option and earnest money must be paid immediately. Most processes being after the option period expires where you will be constantly gather documents for the mortgage loan officer prior to submitting them to the underwriter. Finally, you will receive a closing disclosure, sign closing documents, wire the down payment, and acquire the keys. Let's review the stages of closing.

Initial Payments

After your offer is accepted, there are two fees that must be paid immediately. The first is the options fee and the second is the earnest money. The option fee is normally paid directly to the seller either through a check or wired to the title company. The option fee is paid to the seller and is non-refundable. The earnest money must be wired for same-day arrival to the title company and held in escrow. The earnest money is refunded immediately if you do not purchase the house during the option period. The option fee and earnest money will be a credit toward the final purchase price.

The option period starts the day after the contract is signed.

Inspection

Once the offer is accepted, find a property inspector. Cost can differ by hundreds of dollars between inspectors so I suggest using Yelp and Google to find reputable inspectors. You want a competitively priced inspector that is thorough as well. Agents typically have worked with inspectors in the past and can provide recommendations. Inspectors on average charge $500 for inspections. Your options days are limited, so find an inspector who can perform the inspection within a day or two. The additional option days should be used to estimate damage costs.

If you live in a predominantly warm region that is prone to termites, request for a termite inspection. Termite damage can be significant and ridding a home of termites cost thousands of dollars. Sprinklers can be inspected for additional cost as well. Most inspectors are licensed for both termites and sprinklers. The nominal cost to inspect for termites or broken sprinklers will payoff in the long run, especially if damages are found. Now lets negotiate the damages back into the contract.

Fixing Inspection Issues

After receiving the inspection report, read through it carefully and note the costly items. Costly items include foundation problems, roofing issues, leaks, major appliances like broken ACs, and cracks in the wall. These issues can cost several thousand dollars and impact the property cash flow. Smaller items like aged carpet, paint chips, and other cosmetic issues can be negotiated, but do not let these items prevent a deal.

For costly issues, use the option period to consult a professional to provide estimates. Many contractors will provide free estimates and your real estate agent can provide them access to the home. Also, gather several quotes for each major item. I have had AC companies provide me quotes that differed by thousands of dollars.

For the smaller items, you can contact a handyman to provide an estimate. Handymen can fix many minor issues including carpets, painting of walls, drywall, and light plumbing.

Once you have compiled a list of large and small items prior to the option period expiration, you can negotiate these fixes into the home price. Provide the list to your real estate agent who will negotiate the fixes with the seller. If the seller decides to assist with the damages, they will normally either fix the issues through a contractor themselves, lower the sale price of the home, or provide a credit towards closing. Sellers often provide a credit or lower the sale price to avoid the hassle of fixing the issues. Having estimates for the fixes, allows you to justify the requested amount.

I normally prefer that the seller fix the issues or provide a closing credit, instead of lowering the sale price. Having the seller fix damages is preferred because you will not have to pay for them. A seller credit is the next preferred method for negotiation fixes since the credit is applied immediately to all closing costs. However, the disadvantage is that the credit can only be used towards closing costs and any leftover amount is returned back to the seller. This means that if the damages cost more than the closing cost, the difference is returned back to the seller. Lowering the sale price is the last option, which translates to a small decrease in the mortgage payments and you end up spending thousands of dollars after closing to fix the damages.

Once the seller agrees to fix the issues in the inspection report, your agent will draft an addendum that contains the requested fixes. If the seller agrees to fix the issues, request for all receipts and have your agent do a visual inspection upon closing.

Remember, it is important to get all inspections, damage estimates, and negotiations done during the option period. Being able to walk away from the deal and losing only the options fee, entices the seller to act on your negotiations.

Now that you have finished your inspections, renegotiated the fixes to the home, you are ready to proceed with the rest of the closing process.

Appraisal

The next step in the closing process is the appraisal. A professional appraiser will visit the property and provide the market value given the condition and sales market. Banks will only lend up to the appraised value.

Appraisals begin once the inspections are completed and you intend to purchase the home. Notify your agent and lender so they can order the appraisal. Appraisals costs around $500. If the appraisal is lower than the selling price, you have several options.

1. Pay the difference yourself.

2. Split the difference with the seller.

3. Request that the seller lower the price to the appraised value.

4. The seller can refute the appraisal and review the appraisal for errors.

The option that you pick depends on the market value. In a buyers market where homes are abundant and finding a buyer is difficult, you have more bargaining power and should request for the price to be lowered to the appraised value. In a sellers market where homes sell quickly and buyers are easy to find, the seller may request for a difference split or keep the price as-is hoping that you either pay the difference or they can find another buyer.

I prefer that the seller either lowers the price to the appraised value (Option #3) or review the appraisal for errors and attempt to re-appraise the home to the selling price (Option #4). It might not seem obvious to desire the latter option, but paying differences in the appraisal amount (Option #1 or Option #2), can require additional down payment. For example, if a house was listed at $280,000 and the appraised value was at $260,000, I prefer that the seller lower the sale price to $260,000 or request for the appraised value to be $280,000. Since the appraised value differed by $20,000, even if the seller was willing to split the difference at $10,000 (requiring you to find another $10,000 in down payment), I would rather the home appraise for the additional $20,000 resulting in an increase of $50 a month on a 30 year mortgage.

One of my properties appraised lower than expected, but the seller argued that the appraisal did not factor in the higher quality material and reputable builder when appraising the property. The appraised value was raised back to the agreed upon selling price, which was my preferred option.

Loan Process

Your loan officer will start requesting for documents to prove your income, expenses, and assets. This includes W2s, schedule C, tax returns, bank statements, stock sales, 401K, car payments, and financial statements.

Remember to send your documents promptly for a timely closing. You will spend almost 2 weeks gathering and emailing documents as the loan officer prepares the documents for the underwriter. You may need to provide reasons for income fluctuations, credit inquiries, and significant financial transactions during this time.

Insurance

I have discussed insurance extensively in previous chapters and you will need to finalize the insurance policy at this time. The lender requires insurance on the property on closing day.

Contractors

During the closing process, use this time to find contractors who can prepare your property for rental or home improvements. Contractors can be booked out for weeks and booking ahead of time allows work to begin immediately after closing. Home improvements may include granite installation, appliance repairs, replacing carpets, sprinkler installation, make-ready to prepare the home for rental and any additional fixes that were discovered during the home inspection.

Make-ready is a service that prepares a home for rental. They will perform carpet cleaning, kitchen cleaning, touch up walls and doors, and other fixes needed to get your property to rental code. I recommend comparing prices between companies since costs can vary drastically.

Closing Disclosure

When all documents are submitted and the loan officer forwards them to the underwriter, the individual responsible for reviewing documents and approving loans based on risk analysis, you will be issued a closing disclosure. The closing disclosure contains the break down of the charges for the entire loan process and all amounts owed.

There are often mistakes in the initial draft of the closing disclosure. It will be reviewed by the loan officer and title company. You should also review it for accuracy. Here are some items to review in the closing disclosure.

Loan Terms

Loan terms include the borrowed amount, interest rate, and the exact monthly payments. Check if the monthly payments include property tax and insurance. Personally,

I prefer to pay the property tax and insurance once a year instead of monthly. If the monthly payments include property tax and insurance and you want it changed, notify the loan officer. Note that some lenders provide a slightly better interest rate if the property tax and insurance are paid monthly through escrow.

Closing Costs

The closing cost section include administrative cost to process the loan and also any prepaid items such as insurance and interests. Let's review some of the important items.

Origination charges are the cost to process the loan. You will see discount points that were paid to buy down the interest rate. Double check the rate and discount points for accuracy.

There is a section for *appraisal fees*, which are paid before closing. Since these are listed in the "before closing" column, they will get subtracted out from the final balance. Verify the payment amount for the appraisal, which was ordered during the initial closing process.

Prepaid's include various charge that are due at closing, which includes home insurance and mortgage interest. Verify that the insurance cost is accurate which should match the quote provided by your insurance company or broker.

If you negotiated any seller or lender credits, they will appear in the section *calculating cash to close.* You will see the earnest money deposit that was paid immediately after the contract signing.

There are many other administrative fees that I will not discuss in detail, but they should be straight forward to review. These are fees that lenders charge to process your loan.

Summaries of Transactions

The summaries of transactions section should include the total borrowed amount, the closing costs, and all other fees, which then results to the final down payment. This final amount will be wired to the title company.

One important item is the property taxes that are paid by the current owners. Since property taxes may not be issued by the time of the sale, the lender will use the previous years taxes to calculate the property taxes owed by the seller. The amount owed by the seller will lower the final cash to close. When it comes time to pay the property tax, you will pay the full annual amount.

The "cash to close" is the amount that you will need to wire on closing day.

Signing for the house

After you get the closing disclosure, it gets reviewed for 3 days before the final signing. The 3 days rule is set by the consumer financial protection bureau.

If you are purchasing the property remotely, the title company will send a mobile notary to anywhere at anytime. I have signed for properties at 6am at the comfort of my home. On closing day, you will need a copy of your drivers license and the full cash-to-close amount, which will be wired to the title company. The document signing and review process normally takes less than an hour.

The cash-to-close must be wired to the title company for same-day arrival. After the signing is completed and the amount is wired to the title company, the county needs to record the property to the new owner. The recording often happens on the same day. Once you take ownership of the home, have your agent do a final walk through to ensure that all contractual items are intact.

Congratulations! The house is now yours and it is time to rent it out.

Chapter 6
Getting it rented out

Property Manager

Now that you own the property, you need to sign a contract with your property manager. In previous chapters, I went through the cost involved with property management. Review the contract and ensure that the management fee, leasing fee, and renewal fees are correct. After signing the contract, you will need to fund an account, setup by the property manager, to withdraw for fixes. The real estate agent will need to provide the key to your property manager.

Property managers negotiate their rates and the cost gets cheaper with more properties. I normally check several reputable property management companies for rates and negotiate amongst them. As discussed in previous chapters, you want a property manager who is punctual and responsive.

Your property manager can help you enable the gas, electricity, and water to the home. The maintenance workers will need utilities to begin work. Even if you do not need additional maintenance, the potential tenants viewing your property will need lights. The property manager can pay for the utilities and deduct them from the first month rent.

Maintenance

Even with a newer and well maintained property, you will likely need to perform some minor touchups. Your property manager is responsible for coordinating with contractors to access the home, commonly through a lockbox. For quick repairs, the property manager will accompany the contractor.

You might need your lawn watered and mowed while the property is vacant to avoid a damaged lawn or HOA complaints. Having a mowed and watered lawn will make your property more appealing for potential renters.

Listing the Property

Your property manager will list your home once it is move-in ready. You will need quality pictures of your home to upload into the MLS system. Having high quality photos is necessary to bring more potential tenants. Many tenants determine the homes they will visit based on the description and pictures. Request to see the photos prior to posting on MLS. Once it is published on MLS, 3rd party sites like Zillow and Trulia will pull the photos into their database and any updates to photos could take weeks. I recommend hiring a professional photographer, which only cost a few hundred dollars. Some property managers take poor quality pictures that can drive away future tenants. The additional money spent on better photographs can attract more potential tenants so that it rents out faster and for more money.

With higher end homes, tenants typically have their own washer, dryer, and refrigerator. On lower end homes, tenants may expect appliances. This is region specific so check with your property manager on common expected appliances. Listing a property to include appliances can be attractive to tenants. Even if you plan to purchase appliances, I recommend that you purchase them after a tenant has signed a lease agreement, so you do not end up purchasing appliances that are not needed.

Work with your property manager to determine a fair market rental price. Houses can sit on the market for awhile if listed too high. Using CMAs, compare your listing to similar rentals in the area. You should compare properties that have similar size, floor plans, number of bedrooms, and comparable kitchens. The days on market of comparable rental properties should provide you with a fair market price. Look for prices that took less than 30 days to rent out. Using the prices of comparable homes, calculate a dollar per square feet. You can then multiply the dollar per square feet with your square footage to get an approximate rental price.

The square footage calculation is only an estimate. Many factors can increase the rental value including location, open concept layout, granite counter tops, tall ceilings, natural lighting, and rental demand. Timing is a huge factor since families rent during the summer months once their kids are out of school. The demand goes up along with rental prices. During the fall and winter months, families are less likely to move resulting in lower rents.

One mistake that landlords make is setting a high rental rate and refusing to lower the price. If lowering the rental price by $100 gets it rented out a month faster, you should definitely do it. For example, say you wanted to list a property at $2100, but you determined that it would take 30 days to rent it out. Your other option is to rent it out at $2000, but it would rent immediately. You should rent it out for $2000, since it will take 20 months to make up for the lost rent. Normally, rental rates are adjusted after 12 to 24 months based on the contractual terms anyways.

Once the property manager lists your property in MLS, most of the online portals like Zillow, Redfin, and Realtor.com will show the listing within a day. Now it is time to wait for a potential renter.

Renting it out

Check with your property manager on leads weekly. Proactive property managers will send weekly reports of views and property visits. You will need to make rental adjustments if there is no property visits within a week.

Often times, your property will sit for a week or two without any potential renters. It is advisable to lower the rent in $50 to $100 increments. You should lower the rent weekly until you start getting more traction. If a renter visits, but does not rent the property, have the property manager contact them and request for a reason. You can try promotions, such as 1 month free rent or reduced rental rate for signing a longer term contract if the property continues to sit idle.

When a property manager has found a qualified candidate based on credit checks, credit score, rental history, and ensured that the potential tenants do not have a viscous breed of dogs, you will need to provide the final agreement. Having a viscous dog breed will require you to pay additional insurance.

A contract will be drafted by the property manager when the tenant has been approved. The lease will require the tenant to pay a security deposit which is held in escrow by the property management company. After the lease is signed, the property manager will rekey the property at your cost. Re-keying is necessary to give the tenant a peace of mind.

You should forward mail from your rental property to your own mailbox through United States Postal Service, which is free. Property tax, HOA, and other bills will be mailed to the rental property and forwarded. Remember to switch these bills to your own address because mail forwarding is valid for a year.

Other than waiting for the direct deposit from the property manager, you are all set! Most reputable property manager will have an online portal that shows the cash and balances on the account which is constantly updated.

What else should you do now? Let's find out how to scale, acquire more properties, and protect your personal assets.

Chapter 7
Building your network and scaling it out

After acquiring investment properties, there are a few additional items to handle including protecting your assets, preparing for taxes, and scaling out your rentals. Let's talk through each of them.

Protecting your assets

Protecting your assets is essential in case of unforeseen incidents. You could have trees fall onto your property, someone slips and fall on your sidewalk, your roof could cave in during a storm, or your pipes could burst destroying your tenants property and you may find yourself in litigation. Although uncommon, you need to protect yourself. The more properties you own, the higher probability of an incident.

The 2 fundamentals ways to protect your asset is to create a Limited Liability Company and transferring legal ownership to it or to purchase an umbrella policy insurance. Both have their pros and cons so let's discuss these options. Always consult a real estate lawyer and a CPA regarding these legal protections. Every state has different laws regarding LLCs, their protections, and can vary in cost.

Limited Liability Corporation (LLC)

A Limited Liability Corporation (LLC) is a business structure that provides legal protection its owners. You must consult a lawyer and a CPA prior to transferring your property to an LLC. In terms of real estate, LLCs are used to protect an owners personal assets in the event of a lawsuit against the property. The ownership of the property must be transferred to the LLC.

Starting an LLC is beyond the scope of this book and many states have different processes and costs. Consult a real estate lawyer and CPA to make sure you are setting up your LLC correctly, which provides you legal protection and tax advantages. If you decide to form a LLC on your own, there are many legal websites that help you with the process for a fee. Here are some things to consider when forming an LLC.

If you fully own the property and do not have a mortgage, transferring the property to an LLC is simple. However, having a mortgage makes the property transfer more difficult because of a legal clause tied to mortgages, called due-on-sale. Due-on-sale states that the entire loan must be paid in full upon sale or transfer of ownership. Switching a property to an LLC is a transfer of ownership and some lenders will require you to sell the property or refinance it under the LLC. If you are starting a new LLC, it does not have credit to finance a property. Talk to your lender prior to transferring the title to an LLC, to ensure that the due-on-sale clause will not be executed. You will also need to speak to your insurance company, since the property will be owned by a corporation, and it may be considered a commercial property.

If you are able to proceed with an LLC, you will need to choose the number of properties per LLC. The more properties you have in a LLC, the more assets you will have at risk if litigation arises. Ideally, each property should be in a single LLC, but that can become costly. In some states, each LLC has a minimum amount of tax due, called a Franchise Tax or Annual Fee. In California, this is $800 and will shrink your cash flow. In other states, like Texas, there is no annual fee for an LLC and you can file several series LLC for only a small fee.

An LLC does not protect you against all liabilities, sometimes called piercing the corporate veil. You can be held personally liable if your actions are wrongful or fraudulent.

Another way to protect yourself is with an Umbrella Policy. Umbrella policies are easy to acquire and I recommend having a policy even if you have an LLC.

Umbrella Policy

Umbrella policies protect your assets by providing additional liability insurance on top of your existing rental property insurance. Often times, your home policy will only cover up to $500,000 in liability and your umbrella policy will take over if you are involved in litigation that exceeds that amount.

Call your current home owners insurance and check for available umbrella policies. They are typically cheap and is only a few hundred dollars a year for a million dollar in coverage. You can normally add additional coverage in increments of a million. Insurance companies have a limit on the number of rental properties that can be covered by an umbrella policy. When you reach those limits, you may need to switch insurance companies.

Note, that an LLC and umbrella policy serves different purposes. LLC protects your personal assets from your rental assets in the case of a lawsuit. So if your property is involved with a lawsuit, your personal assets should be safe. An umbrella policy, does not build any barriers between your personal and rental assets. It is an additional insurance on your property that provides financial coverage, in the case of a claim. It is wise to have an umbrella policy in addition to your LLC to protect the assets within the LLC.

Book Keeping

After acquiring multiple properties, the bills and expenses will seem overwhelming to track. Do not worry; all it takes is a little organizational skill.

For each property, keep track of every expense made against that property. This could be lawn mowings, maintenance fixes, property management fees, and traveling expenses. Take a picture of the receipt and upload them into a folder and keep an excel spread sheet of the expenses. You will need these numbers to track your property performance and your accountant will need it for taxes.

HOA payments and insurance occur at various parts of the year. Have a spread sheet available that keeps track of these bills and their due dates. I have HOAs that requirement payments monthly, quarterly, and bi-annually which become difficult to track.

You will need to keep track of rental renewals. During rental renewals, work with your property manager on rent increases to cover for increased expenses on the property. In many states, property taxes are accessed annually and your expenses will increase forcing a rent increase to stay cash flow positive.

Owning rental properties is much like owning a small business. You will need to keep track of revenue, expenses, and figure out how to reduce cost constantly. Organization is a must to run your enterprise effectively.

Scaling out and acquiring more properties

After you acquire your first property and have it rented out, you may be in search for more. Here are a few tips on scaling your enterprise and enable you to acquire more properties quickly.

Watch your Financing

Your debt-to-income ratio needs to stay below 45% to keep borrowing from conventional lenders, whose loans need to follow Fannie Mae guidelines. To continue purchasing homes, you will need to either increase your income or decrease your debt.

Increasing your income means making more money at your primary job or increasing the rental rates. There are no tricks to increasing income. However, it might be easier to decrease your debt, in order to lower your debt-to-income ratio.

Decreasing debt, means spending less money on your credit cards, paying off a car or mortgage, or reducing the expenses on your property. You can decrease debt most effectively by paying off the debt with the highest monthly balance, typically your car payments or credit cards. Reduce the expenses on your property by finding a cheaper property manager, picking a cheaper insurance company, and even ensuring that your property taxes does not increase from year over year. When property tax gets reassessed based on the property value, you can dispute the property tax amount if you believe it is inaccurate. The property tax accessors do not perform a thorough inspection of each property, and can overestimate its value. Disputing that amount will lower your property taxes for the year and reduce the expenses. You can also refinance your loans to a lower rate and extend out the term, which decreases your monthly mortgage and debt.

After acquiring several properties, you will meet all Fannie Mae requirement ceilings and may need to utilize portfolio lenders. Fannie Mae only allows a maximum of 10 mortgages and a 45% debt-to-income ratio. Portfolio lenders however, do not resell their loans to Fannie Mae and do not need to meet Fannie Mae requirements. This does not mean that portfolio lenders have relaxed requirements. They can be more relaxed with certain requirements, such as allowing a higher DTI, but they hedge their risk with higher interest rates, shorter term loans, and higher down payments.

Mortgage brokers can help you locate portfolio lenders.

Make a list of trusted folks

You probably worked with many people in order to achieve your first rental property. You have worked with mortgage lenders, property managers, make-ready companies, lawn care companies, handymen, etc. Now that your lender has all of your documents and financial records, you can get a pre-qualification within minutes and close on another property with only a few updated documents. Then, you can hand off your property to your trusted property manager and fix minor issues with your handy man. Utilize the same people so you do not have to perform the research again. You should find that closing another property is very quick and easy.

Remember to write down the phone numbers and links to the companies of these individuals. When you engage the same individuals for your new properties, you can start requesting for discounts for being a repeat customer.

Diversify your area

Having a several properties in a single area is great because you can leverage your trusted network of individuals.

All of your properties in a single city or area have similar economies, insurance cost, and expenses. If a significant event impacts that area, such as a weather phenomenon, many people will be affected. Similar to the stock market, you should diversify to other states and cities. Many lenders and insurance brokers work across city and state, so they can continue to support your investments.

Invest some properties into slower growth, but high cash flow areas to get consistent rental income. Invest other properties into high growth, but lower cash flow areas to get a potential higher long term payoff. Do not put all of your eggs in one basket.

Summary

After reading this book, my hope is that you can make a systematic choice when investing in real estate. Real estate can provide significant growth on your wealth and tax advantages. It will require a lot of effort to locate the right property and to find the right team to make future home purchases quick. This book hopefully walked you through the steps that you will encounter, in a very concise manner.

I am always available to answer questions so feel free to email me at alan@venturequarters.com. I will be providing additional resources and tools to make your investment simple. Here are additional ways to stay connected.

🐦 @VentureQuarters

📷 @VentureQuarters

f @VentureQuarters

Thanks!

-Alan

Chapter 8
Check List

Before you buy

☐ Learn Cash-on-Cash formula and what constitutes revenue and expenses

☐ Learn Debt-to-Income Ratio formula and what is debt vs income

☐ Figure out a good investment area

☐ Figure out your home criteria

☐ Find a buyer agent

☐ Find a mortgage lender who can provide you with a pre-qualification

☐ Find a property manager

☐ Find a landlord insurance company

☐ Calculate the cash-on-cash potential for properties

Putting in an Offer and Closing on the Property

☐ Calculate the final cash-on-cash

- ☐ Sign the offer

- ☐ Pay the options fee and earnest money

- ☐ Get an inspection on the property

- ☐ Re-negotiate the items discovered during the inspection

- ☐ Order an appraisal

- ☐ Submit all paper worker during the loan process

- ☐ Review the closing disclosures

- ☐ Sign for the property

Getting it rented out

- ☐ Sign contract with the property manager

- ☐ Fix and maintain your property

- ☐ List the property

- ☐ Sign the rental contract

Afterwards

- ☐ Potentially start an LLC

- ☐ Get an Umbrella Insurance Policy

- ☐ Keep track of all your expenses and receipts

- ☐ Watch your Debt-to-Income Ratio for your next property

- ☐ Diversity your properties

27001644R00056

Made in the USA
San Bernardino, CA
24 February 2019